In Dreamscapes Flying

By Chelsea Jahaliel

ISBN: 978-0-6483861-0-0

Copyright © Chelsea Bickley 2018

Chelsea Jahaliel asserts the right to be identified as the author of this work

All rights reserved. No part of this publication may be reproduced, stored in a retrieval system, or transmitted, in any form or by any means (electronic, mechanical, photocopying, recording or otherwise) without the prior written permission of the author.

The author has no control over and does not assume responsibility for any third-party websites or their contents.

Font: Charis SIL, copyright © 2018, SIL International, https://software.sil.org/charis/
This Font Software is licensed under the SIL Open Font License, Version 1.1.

Dedicated to my *she'venyo*, Jamie. I miss you.

Thanks to my tumblr friends – your support means the world to me.

We are the family made by choice,
whose love spans oceans
and we will endure

Acknowledgements

Thanks to @dragonhoardsbookz, @nemothesurvivor, @nelsynoo and @iguanodamn on tumblr for their helpful betas

Also thanks to my husband Chris who ensured all my "i"s were dotted and my t's crossed

Shoutout to thepoetsanctuary.net and verses.net for being home for so many years <3

I. Escaping the Everyday

- *Reality to Fantasy*
- *The Weeper*
- *Silent Music*
- *The First Day*
- *Under Moonlight*
- *Our Stories*
- *Shades of Blue*
- *Man on Fire*
- *What Shall We Die For*
- *The Rose*
- *Dream Beach*
- *Winters Queen*
- *Midnight by Moonlight*
- *Jahaliel part I The Meeting*
- *Suspended*
- *Amethyst Phoenix*
- *Daydream*
- *Forest Sprite*
- *Daring to Dream*
- *Starlight*
- *When the Stars Fell*
- *Sky Maiden*
- *To Grow Wings*
- *Lost at Sea*
- *Old Violin*

I.

Dancing into the teeth of the storm as the clouds break around her
Arms reddened with acid-splash scars that counter pale white lines
Deluge washes away her pain, refreshes her but she cannot forget
Why she does not believe that she's beautiful - heartrending mystery

II.

Archway of jacaranda, interlaced branches create a purple h(e)aven
Above, and below - a lilac carpet mutes footfalls of a mystical sprite
Her dark hair is crowned with the breeze borne blossoms, laughter
Lingers on her tongue, in her eyes tell-tale glitter hints at mysteries

III.

The pale glitter of stars gently light the marble pillared ballroom
Shining down on masked dancers revolving in slow perfect waltz
No words are heard here, save for those spoken by eyes and smiles
Tonight the beauty unbroken, hidden mysteries behind silk masks

I. Escaping the Everyday   Reality to Fantasy

Softly she walks weaving
Her way through paths of dreaming
And her voice rings softly singing
A gentle lullaby

                    Tall she is and willowy
                    Long dark hair flowing freely
                    Flowers of blue adorning her sweetly
                    Tears fall from her indigo eyes

                                    She was dressed in dark gown flowing,
                                    I asked her then not knowing
                                    Who she was, where she was going
                                    I asked her simply why

Her smile she then gifted me
A smile radiant and dazzling
With gentle voice she bespoke me
This thing saith I

                  Tears I shed for the world not knowing
                  The joy of peace that is overflowing
                  So I walk the dream paths always hoping
                  Singing as I cry

                                    For if my tears of joy and sorrow twisted
                                    With my sweet song can make rested
                                    Even one person then I am blessèd
                                    For the tears I cry

As I lay back I assured her quietly
Her singing gave me rest completely
A blanket of moonshine covered me as she
Walked off singing her soft lullaby

Shadows sigh
A magic tower
Beneath the world

Cynic composes
Silent noise
Clouds run overhead

Spectrum scores
Illustrates
Reasons underneath

I. Escaping the Everyday   Silent Music

The furnace roars - fire leaps to freedom, leaving ashes in its wake
Hope dwells in seeds buried beneath the still smouldering embers
When heat is a memory and rain waters the earth, green awakens
And grows - renewed by the rage, strengthened by the destruction

Under soft moonlight silvering our skin
I would dance with you here until dawn
Just you, me, and quietly hummed melodies

All we are to each other is in our eyes tonight
and we are spinning together in a dream
Just me and you until the world intrudes

When you're gone and I'm left alone, I still
dance – pretending like you're still here
that it's me and you waltzing under the moon

Closing my eyes I drift away to where you wait for me
For these few moments you are mine, alas they end
and you must go far from me

If you were real I would hold you forever
If you would return to my dreams I would
love you until we both forget that this is a lie

When morning comes and my alarm clock rings
I have to leave you and every moment away from
you makes me long for evening

Let this reality be our eternal present joy
I could love you, do love you even though
We are merely dreaming of each other again

Sometimes I think on you and me still,
of what we might have been somehow
if our realities had collided instead of
our stories

Dreaming in shades of endless blue
Smoky cerulean, deepest midnight
Swirling together ever deepening
Kaleidoscopic fractals draw me in

Shimmering, twisting, sinuous columns
Of ever shifting cobalt and sapphire
Collapse in on themselves and reform
Into new patterns, delicate and lovely

Midnight hues soften to sky blue
And indigo and aqua dance between
A circle of complimentary changing hues
Ink spilling across smoke, like oil on water

I lose myself in the shifting landscapes
Swimming or flying, maybe I'm falling
But this is a dream so beautiful in blues
I long to remain here, bathed in lapis

Swirling and drifting sweet ultramarine
So many shades and patterns swirling
Never wake, to stay floating through them
Is my desire, to rest in a sea of endless blue

Falling into hellfire, I cried out in helpless pain
When a hand reached out and held on, bringing
Me out from the blaze into a different kind of flame
One that warmed the heart and comforted the soul

He smiled at me, gave me a seat and a cup of tea
Then rushed off to catch yet another soul
Also free-falling, she joined us, and together
We learned again what it was to laugh and love

I had sung magic once before to create a world
My confidence had shattered with its passing
So I curled quietly in the corner, silently watching
As he reached out to so many others and gave life

Did he know how torn I was? I think he must have
He waited and in return for kindness I reached out
Together we built something new on foundations
Of love, strength, trust and hope that will not die

Now we sing together the Fire Man and I
A song of joy that shapes the world anew
Others will come, saved from the burning
And join their voices to our creation chorus

What shall we die for?
That which we live for -
Open seas, free flying souls
Here at the world's end
We'll make our stand
For all we are and will be

What shall we die for?
But what we live for -
the right to choose our love

I hear the swords clash
Winds blow - the storm's a-brewing
Here we shall stand
Here we shall fight

For without freedom,
Where is the life?
Without love, where be the soul?

If it's worth living for,
then it's worth dying for!

So what shall we die for?
That which we live for -
Open seas, freedom to be
And should we die for it
we die in the knowing
Thus ends the beauty of life
Thus ends the beauty of life

A single rose, I watched it grow from bud to full blown blossom
with pain I plucked it from its bush to rest within glass coffin
blood red petals gave way to show its pure centre and I cried
redemption was shown there in the heart washed with gold
burn though my soul does with passion, innocence remains
I will find a way from this cocoon to open up, let love in again
as I moved to fill once more with water the rose's home,
first one
 then two
  then all petals fell
   tumbling to the ground
I wept for the loss of beauty gone so soon after blossoming full
pressed the petals to my heart, smelled the scent of rose fading
at last, crushed, I washed the vase and tossed the petals to the wind

I. Escaping the EverydayA Rose

Early twilight
Stars shine in a violet sky
The water laps gently at the red sand
Colours can be seen by the light of the moons three

Empty beach
I stand at the tide-line
Wading ankle-deep into crystal blue water
Breaking the glassine surface to discover hidden warmth

Dream state
I never wish to wake
Just to stay and play in the sea
With soft sand at my feet and glittering stars above me

I. Escaping the Everyday									Dream Beach

Dressed in midnight and snow, the stars are her jewels
Frost shines in her black hair - over winter she rules

A crown of ice upon her brow, shadows and moonlight her cape
Winds so cold surround her sled and from her there's no escape

She plays the song of winter upon a silver harp
Sings blizzards into being with her voice so dark

Beautiful is she by day and night, lovely is her song
And deadly as arrows bright if you listen for too long

Lonely is the Winter's queen as a far distant star
People who admire her melodies do so from afar

She has feelings just like us and she weeps as she plays
For who would love Winter? She knows no-one will stay

Her lament, her song of cold, freezes the tears she cries
Her only joy is found in the beauty of cloud covered skies

For on each cold winter's night she'll ride through snow and storm
Playing and weeping then going to sleep, hoping to wake never more...

I. Escaping the Everyday   Winter's Queen

A candle outlines a form in a window high
From outside it seems like they are daydreaming
Of a knight or a princess – of the joy of freedom
Able to just be with the one they love

An owl nearby hears the soft huff of a sigh
As the candle is blown out and darkness grows
It takes to the skies with a quiet hoot – a wish
For good dreams and good hunting silently exchanged

She was beautiful – long wavy hair, eyes as changeable as the ocean
With all the grace that freedom brings
With a voice that could charm birds in the trees
She was fond of knowledge, of reading,
Sneaking away to her father's library where
Books of fiction take her away to dream
Where works of science and language allow her to learn
Her mother passed in childbirth,
Her father indulged her in all things, so she grew up
With nature and nurture – a child of forest

One night she was walking out alone,
Conversing with the owls and foxes
When she saw twinkling lights leading along a path
She did not hesitate to follow
In a clearing sat many folk of beauty bright;
A gathering of the Fae – this was
not for her so she turned to walk away,
When a hand rested on her shoulder, and the prince
whispered in her ear "going so soon?"
All her reasoning fled at his nearness

She remembered to murmur "I have not been invited"
"Then come, join us!" He drew her into the crowd
Sat her down beside him and placed choice morsels
Before her – and afterwards when song was called for

She offered up her voice, a gift in return for the food
and she charmed them all – the Fae got up and danced
Save the prince who remained at her side, perfect host
When silver flutes and golden harps took over the music

He offered her his hand, and swept her into the dance
She knew then, her hand burning in his that she was
Falling fast and hard – she did not wish to meet his gaze
She was a mortal human, he was a Prince among the Fae

But he would not let it go so easily –

I. Escaping the Everyday   Jahaliel pt 1: The Meeting

Asking her to speak on what troubled her,
he would make it right if it were in his power to do so,
For he had grown fond of this strange, lovely human -
She shook her head and looked away,
Quiet tears rolled down her cheeks,
He took her hand and led her to a peaceful spot by the cliffs
and once more asked if she would confide in him

I. Escaping the Everyday Meeting   Jahaliel pt 1: The

A frozen masquerade, dancers wait upon their lady's pleasure
Her nails are golden claws, lightning flashes within her eyes
When she steps into the room, music begins, and they dance

She whirls with them for a time forgetting her many cares
Just a masked figure among many, though her dress is finest
They love her, and she loves them; in this moment love is all

Before she has had enough she leaves, duty will ever call her on
But when she passes through the doorway the dancers freeze
They will wait on her return and return she will to this memory

The war that surrounds her in reality makes her dancing deadly
Claws wield swords, lightning pours from her hands, enemies fall
She wishes for peace, she wishes to dance,
She wishes no blood was on her hands

Wishes mean little to Time
And even less to the Power
She is broken but unyielding

She is their Queen

I. Escaping the Everyday   Suspended

In a hopeless world I am the light, fire burns in me ever bright
Shining a beacon of hope that cuts through the darkest night

My wings bear me upwards upon the winds, flight for which I long
When I am at rest, I do not forget the feeling of flying ever and on

❧❧❦❦

Soar high and free with regal beauty, bless those who see thy flight
Stars trail in thy wake as purple fire reveals secrets hidden in night

Never falter, be always blessed, send us justice to fight the shame
Let all the world look up and see the phoenix of amethyst flame

If I could but have this – the dream of mine so simple
to wear a lovely dress and walk into a place owning it
to own a place where musicians can come and jam – the
money we make is from the food and drink, the bands don't
pay us a fee, and sometimes I stay back after closing to
play blues on the grand piano up on the second floor

then if the dream were to change it would grant me
opportunity to travel and meet friends, to change lives
through research, through stories, through gifts

perhaps there would be a special piece of jewellery

or a library filled with the signed copies of friends' books

the dream brings a smile even as reality intrudes
though there are pieces that can be brought to life here and now

if I am but willing to try

I. Escaping the Everyday   Daydream

Once, a little girl wandered into the forest on the edge of the village...

Forget, forget, sweet pretty child
Come and dance, come and dance
Be a forest sprite, wander with us
You are beautiful, come dance with us

Enchanted by the voices she heard, the girl joined the sprites, forgetting who she was, the family she'd left behind

Why do I feel discontent?
I love my home among the trees
For I am a sprite of the forest
Yet I feel something's missing...

Years passed by, until one day she found herself at the edge of the forest

Stare not out at the sun
Dearest come back to us
Come and join in our dance
Do not long after what is outside

This time she did not take heed, and stepped into the light. She aged as she did so, from a young girl of twelve, to a maiden, to a crone, to dust.

For time passes differently
In the forests of the fae
There a hundred years
Is like a single day

I. Escaping the Everyday   Forest Sprite

Dare I to dream
Or will I continue to fade
Drooping like roses in the heat of day

I have nothing
And everything
My path's unclear I can't see where I'm going

Do I dare to hope
Dare I dream you'll be there
Waiting for me at the end of the day

You give me reasons to sing
You give me a reason to dream
You're my light when storms are around me

When I wake from the dream
You are there with me still holding on
My vibrancy is strengthened by the depth of your love

I. Escaping the Everyday   Daring to Dream

Oh how I love you, my starlight!
My love is like a burning fire.
You saved me from darkest night,
and you are my heart's own desire.
In times of trouble I'll not hate
although we may fight at times,
you are the loveliest, happy fate,
deserving of more than glib rhymes.
My commitment to love remains
throughout the passage of the years
With you, I have the world to gain
And naught remains of all my fears

Know this my darling on this day
I pledge, my love, by your side to stay.

The storyteller smiles, a promise of a tale
After sharing a meal, cosy by the fireside
The elder sits and smiles then speaks of when
Stars from the heavens had fallen down

"Once there were countless stars in the sky
Yes, believe me, for I saw them in my youth
Now the stars above were to be a measure of
the wellness of the world down here below

Many years passed in joy and peace, until
Lore of old was forgot – tales told by old folk
and given no mind by more sensible people

I remember though when the star-song faded
a counter to the bodies left out to rot in streets
for a king had arisen, as kings often do, and he
ruled with fear and saw betrayal in corners near
thus the star-song began to cease, their light to dim

We too were diminishing – until one day I saw
a wonder, stars shining bright though it were day
and they fell, singing their songs until none in sky
remained – and despair then covered the world.

Even the king shook in his throne, and I stood
there as though I was stone, remembering the stories
I had been told. They came to me and they were
singing; songs of anger and rage – to war they
were winging, small comforts left behind in their wake

They were a sight to behold, that army of stars
so sharp and terrible in their beauty – they slew
the king, and when peace returned wandered far
they could not return to the skies, they could not
remain here on earth – surrounded as they would
be by lies and the frailness of human love and hope

    I. Escaping the Everyday   When the Stars Fell

None know where they went to – but this truth we hold
should everything once more turn to evil deeds they
will come forth and deliver us, a river of fire and war"

And that is the tale told, you are welcome to stay
The speaker smiles when you take your leave
In the cold night their final words repeat "remember
this: in your life choose to be kind, and you'll do fine"

Clouds shift, forming outline of
a dark blue skinned maiden
with a fiery eye that sees all
Hands raised in supplication
to the moon just above her
reaching out in hope or
in pleading or in prayer

Reminds me of a goddess
kneeling there in the sky
until the clouds start to shift
She vanishes into the night
as I stare at where she was
out of the window as dusk falls

I. Escaping the Everyday						Sky Maiden

I was walking along in the early evening,
Stars out, sunlight lingering in the west
Thinking of all the work there was to do
Wishing for quiet peace and some rest

When all of a sudden I began to glow,
Pain pierced my nerves, muscles tense
Raptor wings of gold and silver flame
Sprung forth, which made no sense

I thought to myself this must be a dream And doubted a moment whether I
could fly but the wings themselves beat at my back
Daring me to let go, to give up control and try

Pushing all thoughts out of my mind, I jumped and I didn't come back down
-before I really knew what was going on
I was soaring high above the ground

In the twilight, guided by the setting sun
I flew over the hills and my cares fell away
The feeling was so powerful and strong
I knew it would always within me stay

I think time may have stopped, while I mastered these wings so beautiful
and I know that I heard the stars sing
The music of spheres so mystical

Eventually I had to return to earth landing unsteady – a controlled fall still,
I know I can fly again if I need
For they remain, waiting on my call

              I dove and there was instant lack of sound
              A quiet peace as water closed around

              Everything was shaded with aqua glow
              Losing track of time I enjoy a world below

              In the ocean deep I watch fish flit by
              Living jewels with water as their sky

I. Escaping the Everyday   To Grow Wings

From the depths I pluck a shell and find it's time to go
So I return to the surface, wonder where did my boat go?

I cannot see it, nor those who dove with me
And while I should be terrified, I feel simply free

Free to open the shell and inside find a perfect pearl
Free to dive once more into the kiss of deep azure

Without doubts and without cares, this is where my story ends
I drift still amongst the waves and current curls and bends

This is truly life, here where peace and beauty collide
Here where even the most shattered soul need not hide

I. Escaping the Everyday   Lost at Sea

Come child listen to an old violin
The music remembers a summer night
Freedom from discontent as the band played
Stars lingered on into day

God was generous to us
Perfect weather, beautiful scent
Of lilies, breath of flowers
Love broke as an ocean around us

Tender smiles
Wedding wishes
Sweet passion
Too brief

Listen to an old violin
The music melancholy tonight
Discontented clouds, rain drips down
Grey world is snowy comfort now

I. Escaping the Everyday   Old Violin

II. Running Wild and Free

- *Fantasy in Colour*
- *The Unicorn*
- *Sketch of a Dryad*
- *Naiads*
- *Hope's Arrival*
- *My Lady Fair*
- *Shared Connections*
- *Heirloom*
- *Fantasy Dreamer*
- *Walker Between Worlds*
- *Leo*
- *Storm-dancer*
- *Cloud Fairies*
- *She*
- *Autumn's Sprite*
- *Moon Dancer*
- *The Second Day*
- *A Silvered Dress*
- *Moiryon*
- *Faded Glory*
- *The Storm*
- *Icarus Falling*
- *Empress*
- *The Four*
- *Return of Winter*
- *At the Theatre*

A queen sits, watches the winds flow by
Using her power to try and open the eye
Of her people who are so wilfully blind
She prays and writes, is truthful and kind

In the hills of the land, magic still dwells
A unicorn blesses a child to grow strong
His helpfulness builds a place to belong
Where secrets are shared (but he never tells)

The winds stir up small sharp sparks into wildfire
Beautiful and terrifying, visions dance in its flames
From the ashes a new and stronger world does arise
And the winds whisper onwards bearing their names

They travel out to sea where they finds a ship, then
Dive far down to see mighty powers of the deep
Whom all sorts of fantastical treasures safely keep
Away from jealous hands and envious hearts of men

A storm brewing once more, grey clouds fill
The sky above a house of laughter and light
That weaves strong magic of love and home
Providing warmth for family against the night

The thunderclouds are pushed into place by
Dragons; scales flash almandine and gold
Elegant and graceful, they own the sky
Breath smoky and warm against the cold

On the stony cliffs on warhorse sits a noble knight
Watching the dragon he was to slay with his might

II. Running Wild and Free   Fantasy in Colour

Knowing in his heart that something's not right
About ending the beauty so wild and untamed

Waiting at home, there's a Lady in purple gown
Watching at the window, face unmarred by frown
She longs to embrace her family, now scattered
Once more for love is to her heart all that matters

From the castle hall a window opens out
To a garden, in spring perfumed by flowers
Though dormant in winter, it's still beautiful
Reminder of hope - seasons change without doubt

Silence of night
Lit by moonlight
A unicorn tosses their head
Dark green eyes shining
They are now pining
For their home and bed

They are trapped
Here on earth instead
Of their world of peace
To try and show
Us who don't want to know
Beauty and kindness at least

They gave us beauty
We gave them despair
Then they faded from view
It seems like no-one knows
That we lost such grace
Remembered as myths not truth

Lithe and glowing with inwards light
Blossoms a crown for her hair
Silver and brown her raiment
She is exceedingly fair

As she walks she is crying
Tears streak her face
For she is lamenting
The fall from grace

Of trees in the forest fallen
Where once they stood tall
Her sisters and brothers
Felled by axe and by saw

Beautiful dryad mourning
Alone in the moonlight
Crying, lamenting
Through the night

When the day breaks
She lets out a scream
Her heart is torn out
Chopped down was her tree

Bubbling brooks of laughter
linger in the air, a chime that
calls you forth from your place
beside the stream to dance
with the naiads fair

boldly they play, rainbows
shimmer in the droplets
flung high into the sky that
linger in the air

carefree dancing, no
uncertain footing in this
stream when they are there

for a while, time pauses
when you join them without a care

II. Running Wild and Free							Naiads

Sweet angel at my door
Beautiful is her smile
Spring blossoms, her scent

Voice like rain
Pouring over my wounds
She is my sanctuary
Protecting my soul

II. Running Wild and Free　　　　　　　　Hope's Arrival

Delicate are her hands
Working patiently at her embroidery
I sit in the corner with my instrument
She dares not notice me

Oh beautiful lady, my only queen
Why were you were born high above me
For if you had been a lovely village lass
Then you I would woo and marry

Eyes the colour of autumn skies
I know that if she were free
All barriers would be overcome
And she would notice me

My queen, you are the only one I love
As I play songs of love, to please thee
Cloaked in the words is my true heart
Belonging to you, for you're all I see

Hair of spun gold and spirit of gentleness
Oh that we could acknowledge this love, be
Able to spend all our days together
I know that you will never notice me

So I'll play for you my fair lady
Your bard, faithful, true to you I'll be
And through the music that we share
I'll find comfort enough for me

It starts with a smiles from old friends and new
With a hundred thousand ideas blooming like
Flowers between our hands - hope illuminates
Manuscript of possibilities in ink shining with
a rainbow of colours so vibrantly alive

It ends with wine and shared laughter
With the shape of future potential
That lights up the sky like stars
Differences are strength we
are not all the same and
that is what makes
our future bright

Blazing chaos filled with light singing song of star bright
Coldest fire with icy flame - dancing death, a fighter's game
My heart's desire fulfilled in thee, no weapon shall I wield but thee
Dragon breath, the hottest flame, shall by thee be clove in twain
Midnight rainbow light and dark with handle of diamond bark
Blade beyond all mortal ken, song of heavens ne'er wrote by pen
And we shall slay the shadows, we shall kill the dead
By us the blood of innocents never to be shed

Your name and story flow in runes on blade writ long ago
You chose me and set me free from dark fate which bound me
You the song, I the singer; you the steps, I the dancer
Beauty together, forever perilous - evil has much cause to fear us
For we shall slay the shadows and we shall kill the dead
We shall seek light and balance until all worlds end

Opposites become one in thee; a sword but a mystery
Elements bow to thy power as we come in darkest hour
No wer, no evil mage, nor darkness in any stage
Shall prevail while thou and I live and breathe star-song's cry
The touch of chaos dark that wends through thy weft and mark
Allows understanding, shakes off fear - no foothold for shadows here
Together we shall slay the shadows and we shall kill the dead
Restoring hope where ever we can, revenging tears that were shed

II. Running Wild and Free   Heirloom

With quill in hand He writes the world
The rhythmic words form quiet heartbeats
His dreams shape beauty from formless ink

The knight upon his horse with mane of gold
Triumphs forth over darkness' army complete
Never wounded, his chain mail missing no link

A quiet strength like uncut diamond curled
Around a warm core of care, the drumbeat
Of music, lent the power to make you think

These are the gifts of the fantasy dreamer, dear friend
May his grace never falter and his dreams never end

Evil is not darkness, yet shadows can be malevolent
wickedness hides itself so well within the light.
Who will stand when control is lost and rules are bent
when power broils in storm so fierce with might?
To cleanse and restore the holiness of the night,
to ensure that the victims are not left helpless,
on any battlefield, to rise up to join the fight
I will stand, sword drawn, sworn as witness.

A child murdered for monetary gain, pieces sent
to a father who in his fierce grief takes up the fight
and changes the shape of the world, no longer pent
his anger - gone beyond rage, tears blinded his sight.
A woman who is broken in spirit and left to soul-night
many face harms unspeakable and cry out in silence.
The pain will never be healed, oh how that does bite
I will stand, sword drawn, sworn as witness.

To repay violence with violence seems insolent
but the blood of innocence cries out in the night.
To honour and protect was what my vows meant
bringing all my strength and weapons to fight.
Kill the evil and all who serve the corrupt right,
to avenge, to judge and then wounds to dress
saving what I can, restoring faith in dark and light.
I will stand, sword drawn, sworn as witness.

I am Guardian; I am fire and searing light,
the walker between worlds all wrongs to address.
Wherever are troubles, evil and fear in the night
I will stand, sword drawn, sworn as witness!

Bright white teeth,
a star lion shining.
Past the waters' surface he marched
Leading silent problems over
the world's cool black skin

II. Running Wild and Free   Leo

Teasing breeze tugged at her hair
Wanting zir to join the dance
Lightning played above in the sky
As rain coated zir skin like glass

When ze danced the wind was zir partner
The open grassy fields zir ballroom floor
Sound of thunder and rain were the band
With lightning bright, who could ask for more?

Storm dancer spun and twirled in time
To the music of the rain that fell
While all others hid at home in bed
Ze was out, caught in the storm's spell

When the storm had passed over
The wind released with a sigh zir hair
Then the moon and stars shone again,
As ze walked home without a care

Using a cloud up high for a platform
They jump and dive
d
o
w
n
towards the earth
High trilling laughter floats on the wind
As they perform
tumbles and flips, trailing ice
Behind them as they fall,
nearly
to
the ground
Then the wind blows and they ride the breeze
Soaring back up to the next place in the line
Waiting impatiently to jump back down

Smoke rises from the floor as shimmering lights shift in glorious patterns

breathe in
breathe out

Anticipation swells and breaks
with a thunder crash of toms
rising bass reverberates through
the floor sinking beneath our skin
through all of this she dances
each step timed to pick out the rhythm
of the drums – her arms move loose and
languid, a total lack of self-consciousness
her quick steps enchant me
I lose my breath to the way
her gold-fire hair shines, her
slow slides, the sinuous curve of her back
I'm falling a little in love right now
in this club with its smoke and sound
I want to join her, to counter her
steps and to move freely as we
dance as one effortless flowing from
song to song without a pause in motion

Breathe in
Breathe out

Everything is warmth and music and motion, our smiles shine
brighter than the spotlight

II. Running Wild and Free					She

Autumn's sprite dances through the forest
Painting the trees with russet and gold

In his steps a cool breeze follows
as he dances in falling leaves

Animals begin to find warm shelters
he scatters nuts and grains to store
into their path, the last harvest

The rains are coming, the nights turn
Cold in contrast to his colours warm

In a forest far away Autumn's sprite
Dances leaving colour behind in his wake

Flowers in their hair
Through light and shadows
Dancing without a care

Dancing without a care
Moving to their inner tempos
A breeze stirs the evening air

Flowers in their hair
Soft cool moonlight shows
Their lissom body bare

Dancing without a care
Their supple grace flows
The gentle rain their pair

Flowers in their hair
Through both heat and snow
They are always dancing there

They are quite unaware
Guileless, beautifully so
Dancing without a care
Flowers in their hair

We dance, the music coming up from the floor reverberating through our feet
Faster and faster, an endless loop of bass and drums as we move together
One unit - spinning and smiling and laughing even as your edges fall apart
Within one beat and the next you vanish into smoke, an illusion broken

I am alone, but at least for now I still smile

II. Running Wild and Free   The Second Day

Soft and gentle, flowing and yielding
I know appearances can be deceiving
For such I appear as beauty and grace
And it would seem that's my only face

Grey so gentle, lined with silver fair
A dress designed for style and flair
Hidden secrets lurk in my curves
To help her get what she deserves

I appear soft but can turn sharpest blade
An edge to pierce me has not yet been made
My wearer has no restrictions on movement
To fighting as well as dancing I am lent

When I watch her and I in the mirror
I would smile, if I could, in wonder
For here is beauty, power and deceit
Handful of secrets for my wearer to keep

II. Running Wild and Free   A Dress of Silver

I walk in the storm's heart with eyes of lightning
Voice of the pouring rain and crashing thunder

When the springtime comes I renew the earth
My hair is the dark clouds which cover the sky
And when I dance the wind blows wild and free

Revered for my power, I create raging winter storms
Loved for life giving water in the autumn and spring
Longed for in the summer months - I am weakest then
But when I am remembered by people, then I live again

I have been cursed by beauty
None who see me think of power
They think my blood can heal

Fools, my whole self is the healer

Power for destruction
Where evil reigns
Power for peace and joy
And the life giving dance

I am misunderstood by so many
Seen as a chance for monetary gain
I will forsake this world

Find heaven where there is no pain
That cannot be healed by a touch
No anger and no fear

Away from this world where I
Have been so misunderstood
But I am not so cruel
As to leave them without dreams

An illusion, a whisper on the wind
Is all I will leave of me

Child of storm xe whistles up the winds
Laughs as lightning cracks purple-white

Xe dances in the summer deluge
Fears not the bruising hail of winter

Xyr pain brings down the bitter rains
And xyr fury the maelstrom creates

Xyr smile is the rainbow and the sun
That shines through the thunderheads

II. Running Wild and Free   Faded Glory

With face upturned xe lets the rain soak
Into xyr skin and delights in xyr power

II. Running Wild and Free   The Storm

Given wings of feathers and wax to soar
and find a sun – to fall to the sea for
what they claim as arrogance
but you were blinded by
his beauty and flew
closer to see
how he
glows
falling
you don't
drown because
he is laughing and
offering you a hand when
you take it your wings reform in
golden sunshine and you are flying with
him into a paradise that tales will never tell

In skies of aquamarine and silver
Firebirds leave trails of golden stars
She catches one on her palm

With a song, clouds shed their tears
Drops stream to refresh the ground
She catches one on her palm

With a whisper of magic they fuse
the gold and the silver into one
A ring rests on her palm

Whispers by her people in the night
Their prayers and hope for daylight
Heard through the ring from her palm

The four beings complement and complete
To dance with them is life and death for all
Who draw breath – fire's bright crackling
Laughter can steal the oxygen from your lungs
But there is none as entrancing as they to watch
And the sunlight on the water is a path leading
Astray but how many souls long to step on and follow
Air's sweet songs of wind in the trees, a perfect mix
That allows us to thrive, though their anger is feared
Finally Earth, sweet and caring – portrayed as provider
loved for the way that they never give up, always return
nothing we build will outlast them, the spirits of elements

Sunlights fading caresses the earth with golden light
The river wends slowly waiting for the rains of renewal
Wind blows cool, the air is fully of chilly stars, diamond pinpricks
The colour of the leaves is turning, changing from verdant to russet

And as the world dances on through the seasons
She waits at the edge of the world for summer's end
Platinum hair, midnight eyes - Winter's king stares down
From the icy mountains where he lives all year round

"Soon," Autumn whispers, "soon he will ride down to the plains
And bring snow and frost til just a mem'ry of summer remains"
She changes the colours of the leaves and sweeps the off the trees
Shortening the days, stirring up an early storm, warning of what is to come

For a season he will reign over the earth in white
And deep will run the river underneath its crust of ice
The bitter winds will keep the people tucked inside their houses
Remembering the warmth of Summer and wishing it back again

Audience hushes slowly, as lights slowly fades
Balconies fill with mink coats and diamonds fair
Conductor quietly signals the orchestra to begin
Dramatic strings and bold brass sound the notes
Entwined through the opening bars of a mystery
For tonight we watch, laugh, and cry at the show

Graceful entry stage left, soprano putting on a show
Her voice rings out full and clear as the music fades
Into the backing for opening number of the mystery -
Joined together, song and singer, each wondrously fair
Kindness of my neighbour who lends me program notes
Lost in wonder I try to find words, but where do I begin

Music draws to a close, the interval to begin
Now we mingle, this too is part of the show
Ogling the beauties while reporters take notes
Pictures of stars remain as performance fades
Quickly resume our seats, the curtain opens, fair
Rosalie sings, luring us once more into mystery

Such a plot, there's a beauty to this mystery
That reaches through song and dance, begin
Unravelling the threads as on stage a funfair
Very quickly takes place, a show within a show
Wakes the characters to the solution, scene fades
Xylophone chimes start of final act, tuneful notes

You get lost in the music, in the sweeping rise and fall of notes
Zane murdered Stefan in jealous rage, revealed the mystery!
Arrested and ashamed, now he hangs his head as light fades
Before returning stronger as the finale's about to begin
Chorus of many voices revel in the power of love to show
Devious deeds for what they are, how justice makes life fair

II. Running Wild and Free   At the Theatre

Evening turned to late night while watching this musical fair
Finally the applause and encores fade, echoes of notes
Ghost in the air, remaining long after end of the show
How great it was, we all enthused, a musical mystery
I've been inspired, says a friend, take me home and I'll begin
Jokingly to write my own music, to ensure this memory never fades

Kidding around we begin the journey home, seeming now so fair
Lovely moment fades but will bring back joy when smile fades
Music ringing on the notes play still in my head such a mystery

III.   Shifting Nightmares

- *Electrum*
- *White Wings*
- *Weep with Me*
- *Lady of Grey*
- *Fading Twilight*
- *A Lament*
- *Without Love*
- *Hope Fades*
- *Dream*
- *Catching Drops in Bitter Glass**
- *Celestial Nightmare*
- *Running from Lions*
- *Guilt Trip**
- *Jezebel*
- *This Nightmare Life**
- *Shadow Lurker**
- *Curse the Day*
- *Beautiful Nightmare**
- *Waking or Sleeping**
- *Lady Death*
- *The Price of a Name*
- *Soul Eater*
- *Eyes of Madness**
- *Remember When*
- *Dance With the Devil**
- *Time Eats*

This section deals with dark and distressing themes – the nightmares that are so often part of the dreamscape. Please use your judgement on whether you read these works.

Pieces in the contents of this section marked with an asterisk contain very mature themes including descriptions of self-harm and suicide. They are also marked with a row of * at the top of their pages.

beyondblue.org.au is a good site with help and information on mental health.

III. Shifting Nightmares   Electrum

Foreboding clouds of darkest grey
Pierced by golden shafts of light
Through the holes you can see
Silver linings, a reminder of good

In my dreams I see a sword of silver and
Gold dragons soaring in skies of crimson

Sometimes I fly on angel wings, other times I fall
Into the void as darkness swallows tears of crystal

Sail away on the wind
Tears become the rain
White wings carry me
To a land that's far away

Heart of lead feels like
A millstone around my neck
I wish to tear it out of me
On the rocks below let it wreck

My tears will water earth below
My breath falters, life I cannot see
Unless these white wings of mine
Can bear this load and carry me

Forever I fly trying to escape fate
Lonely and tiring of my tears
There's no land of rest for me
Just painful loss and fears

Weep with me, come mourn with me
For talent passed beyond this life
Raise a tribute in pouring out of song
Tribute to the master, who is dead and gone

Weep with me, mourn with me, come
Ah! Why did the fatal blow fall
Upon the proud bard standing tall
Where is the justice in the death of music's light

Weep with, come mourn with me
For he never made it safely home,
Never got to say goodbye to his family
Unreconciled he passed beyond knowing

Mourn these days we live in
Where freedom is but a lie
And justice need only apply
to those with coin to afford it

Weep with me for spirit and talent lost
Join the wake with his successor who mourns
In sorrow raising song for the passing of a friend
Whose music lit up years of darkness

Weep for the mysteries unfulfilled
Cry for the passing of the light
And all that was lost to the falsehood
Which calls itself "justice" and "right"

Weep with me, come mourn with me

          The mists blow in from the waters
          Cold veil that adorns the mourner
          She screams out her rage and sorrow
          A lament that breaks the hearts who hear

          Her tattered raiment was once fair
          Alas - the world intruded into
          The sanctuary of her peace, destroyed
          What her regard had held as holy

III. Shifting Nightmares   Weep with Me

Now she has nothing left to hold,
Nothing that can contain her anger
When her sorrow fades to the passing
Days, all that will be left is vengeance

Where she walks and weeps
Her tears fall and scar the ground
As though they were an acid rain
Nothing will be allowed to grow anew

Watery moonlight coats the world in pale silver
As fading colours on the horizon wash out to blue
Stars silently shining, faint diamonds in the ether
Clothed in twilight's glory I stand alone, missing you

Dusky indigos and violets streak across the top of the sky
Wind blows cold, the birds and flowers are going to sleep
The zephyr's caress reminds me that time is passing by
Surrounded by nature's beauty my lonely soul does weep

III. Shifting Nightmares					Fading Twilight

Sing out, you harps, a lament for the living
Scarred from the experiences overseas
No medication, no money can ease
Wounds of the mind beyond healing
Remember the ones that fell, remember them
But also think of the ones who came home
Whose life was no longer their own
Nightmares and horrors ever plagued them

Sing, harps, sing! These ones bought for us
Freedom that most precious gift
At the price of their wellness, no justice,
They hate the fact they returned, a rift
Between them and their families
Let us always remember these

III. Shifting Nightmares   A Lament

In a city where everything seems to be desaturated
People go through their lives in almost automation
Streetlights dim the stars but there's safety behind
The Wall - a safety given at such a small, small cost

Within the Wall there is no love - no families, no
Partners, no relationships at all beyond those you
Work with, and this robotic atmosphere protects
You from all that lies out there in a world gone mad

You leave behind everything that makes you unique
Step away from those you cared for, let go of your lover
Your child, your family to go to separate areas but you
Will never go hungry again, never have to fear the riots

Many who live there receive lobotomies, remove that
Which is forbidden and they are lauded for the decision
But some struggle with it, some think about leaving
(though the Wall doesn't just keep the outside out)

Some believe that this is wrong - that they were made
To love, to care - to be more than this pale world can
Hold, and sometimes they reach out to find another
Like them - a sign: curved forefinger and straight thumb

There's a danger to it - should they be caught they
Will be given three options - death, lobotomy or exile
With nothing save perhaps a suit of rags if the Seniors
Are feeling generous; this is the risk they run willingly

III. Shifting Nightmares   Without Love

Hypothetical flutes
renew stiff air.
Their whistling
warrants memory...

Faithful darling
Desirable
Admirable
She listened

...frequent hope
explodes
in horror

It is over

Once I walked through a building
carrying something metal in a bag.
There was (for reason unknown)
a gas leak spreading through the air.
I moving fast, trying to escape
when I tripped and dropped the bag.
A spark, a decision… Explosion.

I was lying face down on the ground;
amazed I wasn't dead from the pain I felt.
The scene changed, I was in a hospital room
decorated as if it were my childhood space.
The nurse came in and said I'd live,
but my scars would be terrible unless
I had cosmetic surgery to fix them

(I didn't really care for that idea)

Not just the scars she urged,
while you're here and need help
have reductions and enlargements
to make you worth something again.
I told her no, and argued long
that I'd be loved anyway.
My mother came in and told me
I looked hideous, she'd disown me,
so I should be good and have the surgery.
I thought of you, and held that thought -
you said you'd love me no matter what.

Would you love me scarred and broken?
I wondered as my eyes opened

****

> *"That's a lovely necklace you're wearing*
> *I've never seen gems that shade of red*
> *How deep and rich the well of colour is*
> *Within them, as if they were liquid inside "*

III. Shifting Nightmares   Dream

I smile

Sharp shard of mirror across a vein
Open up and pour it out to frozen air
Catch the drops in cold molten glass
Forming beads the colour of crimson

I weep

Bitter glass, bitter smile
Necklace worth the while

I am envied for the beauty of the beads
Around my neck while my heart bleeds

III. Shifting Nightmares   Catching Drops in Bitter
Glass

Her hair is black flame blown by winds of the ether
Galaxies are born, dance, and die in fathomless eyes
She glows with a beauty unearthly, dressed in scarlet

Full luscious lips bring carnal promises to mind
Closer inspection reveals their sharp edged cruelty

She haunts the dreams of young men, promising lust
should they give in she becomes the incarnate of wrath
No mercy in her eyes, no forgiveness in an immortal soul

Celestial nightmare weaving her patterns through dreams
in the plane of unconscious thought nothing is as it seems

III. Shifting Nightmares											Celestial Nightmare

Swirling mist drags me into a black spiral glittering with stars
As it fades from my eyes I see a stark and broken landscape -
Clearly no hero has arisen to save this place from destruction

I run, wanting to escape the hopelessness that surrounds me in this desolation,
tempting me to despair; I collide with a body, breathless, we stare at each other
Wariness in my eyes and movements I begin to withdraw, he pulls out a badge
Blurry yet familiar the lines, the shape of it - but I cannot trust - not him, not now

When he reaches out again I whirl and run, prompted by a feeling deep inside
With a roar of frustration, the man becomes a lion chasing me to devour my essence
Like he has devoured the essence of this land, but even as I run I realise the truth

That holy knowledge fills my veins like sparkling wine; new strength infuses me
Opening my mouth I sing as I run, my song calls forth new life in riotous colour
Without breaking stride I leap into the multi-hued mist and ascend from the depths
Waking, I hear echoes of frustration roaring in my ears but here he cannot reach me

III. Shifting Nightmares   Running With Lions

****

Sitting by herself, the door is locked
in her hands a knife

It's a pretty thing, sharp too
Handle inlaid with quicksilver
Given to her for her birthday

Today is the anniversary, nine years of not wanting to live
Because they died, because of her

Guilt tripping just once a year
Although the pain is constant
A thin red line appears on a leg
Already covered in scars

She wants to feel pain, not to kill,
No, that would be the easy way out
It's her fault and so she must bleed

What ifs run though her head, the knife leaves patterns on her leg
she whispers names to the empty room

Pain eases the guilt if temporarily,
The silent ceremony completed
Another set of guilty scars to hide
When tears are what she needed
But could never find

Trailing silk dyed with blood she spilled
Where she walks death follows at her side
Atop her golden hair, a crown of bright bones
Damned she walks alone, her greatest sin - pride

The world turned its back on her
Now she spins it on her little finger
Demon-goddess incarnate, seven sins
Each gave her twisted blessing to linger

She kissed the dragon of the dawn
And burned with fire black and gold
No room in her for love or mercy
To be great she must be ice cold

Wrath and Lust make her passion dangerous
Envy and Sloth gave power at the cost of sanity
Gluttony gave her desire for endless baubles
Her renowned beauty a gift of sweet Vanity

And Pride, pride started it all
With one kiss innocence burned
What was left in the wake was Jezebel
Mighty queen, from human to demon turned

Silent screams as emotions stretch, then the sudden snap
Leaves behind a broken shell watching her soul take flight
Music stops, not even the drumming of her heart remains
Dreams twist to nightmares, rivers of blood flow this night

III. Shifting Nightmares   This Nightmare Life

****

Don't sleep without the doors all locked
The blinds all shut to keep out the night
In the shadows waits the nightmare man
THE SHADOW LURKER

He plots and plans his attacks
And then when they are done
He'll come peering in your windows
He'll be knocking at your doors

He'll say something innocent -
Needs to borrow a cup of sugar
And if you let him in it's all over
He'll take *good* care for you

A twisted truth that should scare you:
He can make you enjoy what he does
You'll never be alone for the rest of your life

Forever love and forever hate
the shadow lurker; he is your fate

Summon the night and curse the day, rain blood down on corrupt land
Let fangs pierce all that remains of innocence, drown the feeble dreams
Screams will fill these ears with joy, come now dance to the end of time
Share this pain in sick parody of love; let the darkness make you mine

****

Fractured rainbows
Shimmering tears
Forgotten fears

Sharp edged mirrors make the skirt
Hair coated with diamond-glitter dust
Taken from the shattered chandelier

Jagged edge
Purest glass
Dancing shards

I am silent, with nothing to sing for
I cannot feel, except for remorse
That you would not leave me be

Keening tears
Lost in reflections
Death is not my fear

III. Shifting Nightmares   Beautiful Nightmare

****

In the day I am alone
Hiding in my corner
Fearing what will come
When the sun goes down
For in the night though I try to stay awake
My eyelids slowly droop, sweeping me away
To my twisted dreams, where nothing is as it seems

I can hear screaming, I recognise the voices
I cannot see, I cannot speak and all I know
Is that I am helpless, trapped within a cage
While the ones I love are in pain and dying

So I long to wake up to end this torment
I force my eyelids open and try to catch my breath
Know that if I never want these dreams to manifest
I must not let anyone close, I must shut all the doors
Nightmares haunt my sleep
Loneliness crushes my waking
I would rather die...

I would rather die, there's a thought
Death would be an end to the torment
For the terror of these prophetic dreams
Blight my life whether awake or asleep

Hush my love, don't cry
Let my cold bones embrace you
Draining your flesh of vitality
Melt into my kiss and drown

See her standing in robes of crimson dark
Leaning on a black-wood and silver scythe
She will sweep a harvest of souls tonight

Betrayed, beloved soul, I can show you
The intoxication of desire where the fall
From pleasure will never end, descend
With me into the velvet warmth of death

The armies pray to Lady Death that she
Takes only their enemies, but she doesn't care
Whose blood is shed, it is souls she seeks to keep

Foolish, rushing to your end, come then
Dance with me on every plane, feel me
Around you - for one moment your blood
Revives me, you'll die remembering my touch

The terror of her beauty does not stop them
For to dance with Lady Death is to gamble between
Pleasure and despair; in the end only she is left standing

There are no words left for me
Each has been stolen away
Now I live eternally dying
The price of my freedom too high

Evil has taken me into its embrace
All I was lost to its hunger
now I wander this hell
With anger my clarity, death my heart

The shadows mercilessly left a reminder
Of who I was before I challenged him
I scream with no words, a desperate plea
To scare others away from becoming like me

It grows stronger with each who fails
I was foolish to think I would prevail
If this hell could it would break free
And none on earth would survive it

So each night I scream...

Enchanting smile
Smile of a thief
Thief of souls
Souls of people
People caught by his charms
Charms from another realm
Realm of vivid nightmares
Nightmares beyond imagining
Imagining the sharp tooth smile
Smile of a siren or some such
Such a sweet seeming thing
Thing with their own agenda
Agenda to do more than survive
Survive by feasting on death
Death of unwary people
People that lose their souls
Souls to his enchanting smile

III. Shifting Nightmares				Soul-Eater

****

Unflinching gaze commands absolute attention
Like a serpent's hypnotic stare, his eyes demand it
And a voice whispering in my ears, "I know all your secrets"
"Betray your friends and I will end your suffering"

Limply, I hang in chains that bind me, trying to resist
Though my throat is raw with screaming
I know that he will not desist

Eyes of madness, let me drown, sinking down to find
A place free of pain where those eyes cannot read my mind
Where the voices cannot corrupt my ears

Impatiently he begins anew and rough hands jerk up my head
Meeting his gaze, I know I cannot deny him for much longer
Even though I would rather die, my broken body will betray me
For it clings to life and the promises in the eyes of my captor

Memories of those I love crowd at the door to my mind
I will not give up their names for him to find
And in sorrow I know there will be no rescue

Eyes of madness, I will not submit! And with one last breath I sigh
Spiral down and inward and trip the key to my own death, I cry
Once more, "I will not submit!"

III. Shifting Nightmares   Eyes of Madness

I came to you with nothing but innocence and a bag of silver and stakes
Oh, how you lured me with your siren's beauty, chained me with your words
How well I remember the moment when the sharpened wood fell from my grasp
And you kissed me, your fangs pierced my vein and for a time all was dark
I awoke to your embrace, we were tangled together - limbs and silken sheets.

We ruled then, in a world that feared and hated us, we were empresses
We went to war to drink the fear of men, to crush them beneath our heels
I still taste the blood that spilled into our waiting mouths, how we loved to share
How the bloodlust turned to pure lust, our frantic pleasure melding together
Incapable of gentleness, still such love was enough for the shards of my soul

I loved you then - I love you still, though we are shadows of our former glory
Though they try to kill us off, we are a never-ending story

III. Shifting Nightmares					Remember When

****

Hold me
d
  o
    w
      n

and kiss me hard
burn me up, bite my lips

                                            (til I **bleed**)

in your eyes the fires

  a n
d   c   g
      i n

There will be hell to pay for this night
But your arms are full of illicit delights
So touch me, let lust-fire burn my wings

wanting me

Tonight I'll dance with the devil
And I'll lose my soul to pleasure
With a final glance
p
u

I step clear of the ashes of innocence
And fan the crimson flames of this passion 'til I die
I will let you pull me down
                                      (take me now)

In-between breaths a thousand
stars fall in a bright flash;
between beats of a heart
Obsidian crumbles to dust.

Remnants of ruins fade
into desert winds and the
sands scour flesh, abrading to
bone which in time returns to
the earth - darkened grave
of queen(s), tired and broken.

Powerful and unbending in life
time was their undoing, in the
storm - a flash of lightning; an echo
of laughter but it is not her, not them...

Nothing left but the after-image:
red-stained hems, skulls under feet.
Thousands died for love of them -
between one beat of a heart
and the next - the world is gone,
Time feasts and then moves on

IV. Eternal Breath of Dawn

- *The Fire*
- *Prismatic Dream*
- *Jahaliel part 2: The Wedding*
- *Hope Renewed*
- *Eventide*
- *Echo*
- *Stars and Flowers*
- *Starlight Kisses*
- *Crystal Flowers by Moonlight*
- *Imagine*
- *Phoenix Dreaming*
- *With You*
- *Nameless*
- *Calling of the Stars*
- *The Creators*
- *Starry Eyed and Dreaming*
- *Dancing with Muse*
- *See the Sea*
- *I Dream*
- *Dawn-Bringer*
- *A Proposal*
- *The Fourth Day*
- *Upon a Distant Hill*
- *Endings*

Screaming as they burn so bright
Words dissolving into their letters
One by one vanishing into smoke
Lighting up the darkened night

In the fire pictures shift and grow
From the word-wood, and to me
It is a phoenix, sparks in their tail
Rebirth of the story burning low

(Shifting and ever changing games
Blues within, oranges shining through
The pictures and the burning words
Form beauty which is poetry in flames)

Along the horizon mountains of citrine and amethyst gleam
As sapphire moonlight refracts through the star filled sky
Ruby tulips nod their heads in time to the melodic wind
Striking chimes from the trees in all their glittering glory
Such beauty would make the fair folk, even the gods weep

and through this I wander

Every breath changes the lights that surround my form
Lost in crystal becoming reflections; a rainbow of light.
Gentle joy consumes all the aches and cares I ever felt
I dissolve into a mist that becomes a song in the wind

I touch the mountains and the ocean

My breath is felt by the topaz trees and the emerald grass
Each element I touch changes the song, refining the melody
Rainbow motes soar and scatter through the crystal heart
No end, no beginning, an endless reflecting kaleidoscope

I lose all thought, will to never wake from this prismatic dream

IV. Eternal Breath of Dawn   Prismatic Dream

Into depthless eyes she fell, compelled to speak the truth of the love she felt, so suddenly fallen
into – that pain of distance between a human and someone like he
Turning then to leave him to the company of his own – she was held fast once more
by his hand, "please listen to me" He asked, she nodded, numb
heard Iargail speak of love and sorrow beyond human comprehension

Yet he returned her love – she trembled as he leaned in
waiting for her acknowledgment before kissing her with abandon
They agreed to meet again beneath the full moon and there pledge themselves to each other with
joyous heart she danced on home to craft herself a wedding dress
from gifted petals delicately preserved sewed by her own hand to create a beauty
That would match that of her beloved's – even as she worked, Iargail spent time trading favours
until he had two circlets – one for each of them, a sign of troth

Under the light of the moon in the company of great Fae
and small they recited the vows of marriage, grinning all
the while, for this was an expression of their true desire
Silver graced her brow, placed there by her Prince
She sung a song of love to him and only him, then they
Feasted with music and laughter and the joy of the dance
A nectar sweet was prepared for her, that she might drink
of it and spend forever with her beloved – and drink she did

Dawn saw the lovers alone, she whispered that she should say farewell to her father Hurrying
back to her former home she saw a carriage pull up, guests she suspected,
Until her father revealed that the woman was his new love someone he cared for,
not a replacement for her mother but she would ease the loneliness in his soul

She breathed out relief that he wouldn't be left alone, told him of her marriage,
that she would be leaving to likely never return again – he gave his blessing and love
She saw Iargail awaiting her and ran laughing to him – swept up and kissed soundly
so they left with their company fair for the forests of the fae, and together there lived

IV. Eternal Breath of Dawn   Jahaliel pt2:The Wedding

Flutes whistle...

A fairy listens
She emerges, north void's daughter
Wandering
Renewing the faithful
A memory

Hope

Listen,

flutes are whistling...

IV. Eternal Breath of Dawn   Hope Renewed

Look up unto heaven and see shining light
Hear songs of stars drifting down to caress
The rain scent lingers a whispered promise
Warmth vanishes under blanket of night
Moonlight shining, pearlescent glow around
Dance now and the sorrows flee far away
Under heaven, stars distant music play
And lift your spirit far above the ground

Eventide, sweetest time of day or night
With joyous dance swallow up my sorrow
In this moment where fire and ice do meet
Joining the unity of bright and fading light
Let come whatever will when it is tomorrow
For this night, rest now safe and complete

Red Queen stands on the cliffs of her kingdom
Sends out love to a long forgotten sister
The seas and skies echo with the cry
"I love you"

Shadow King within obsidian walls
Sits and writes, as long dead heart seeks
Comfort, echoing through lonely rooms
"I love you"

Heart-master watches as the sun sets
Stars shine and holding breath he lets
Out words that echo the world through
"I love you"

Man of words in silent tomb
Waiting for his endless doom
Is refreshed by echoes invading
"I love you"

White Queen stands on sandy beach
Wondering about family long out of reach
From her heart an endless echo begins
"I love you"

Hearing a voice of love, encouraged, I jump
Falling past stars - dizzy with spinning lights
Spirograph images form around my head
Praying as I fall for a landing that is soft
Alas my fall is arrested by a bed of flowers
With thorns holding impossibly sharp edge

Diamond bladed saw ne'er had such an edge
As those flowers I landed on - in pain, I jump
There is nowhere to go except back to the flowers
The stars shine, mocking me with their lights
They are hard and distant, I am present- soft
So I bleed from the many cuts to my head

I raise my hands to my aching head
I realise I am lying near the edge
Of a cliff covered with nothing soft
My body reacts to my emotion, jump
Once more trying to reach the lights
Of stars, reflected in petals of the flowers

Ah, but they were lovely those flowers,
 colours I never saw except inside my head
Their centres contained sparkling lights
I forget in their beauty the cutting edge
And reach once more, risking the jump
Hoping that in my hand they will be soft

They lie, those stars, they are not soft
They are naught but illusion of flowers
And now I am scared, running, I jump
Away, let me away, I scream in my head
For my voice has no sound, no cutting edge

IV. Eternal Breath of Dawn   Stars and Flowers

Here in this garden of shifting lights

I want the darkness to cover these lights
Stars and flowers neither can be soft
I cannot escape, trapped on the edge
They cut me endlessly, these flowers
Here I am trapped within my own head
Remembering the cliff I run and jump

Edge of nightmare receding slowly, I wake, hold my head
Soft love receding, all my joy has faded like the star's lights
Jump whispers the voice, but I won't be cut again by those flowers

IV. Eternal Breath of Dawn   Stars and Flowers

tender warmth
caressing hair and face
starlight kisses
joy in sweet embrace

to lose oneself
to the warmth of
starlight kisses
more joy than words

begin anew
the dream of
starlight kisses
together, there is joy

Silvery light turns a garden into a fantasy dreamscape
I hold in my cupped hands the most delicate flower
Its petals are soft, and it smells of jasmine and spice
Clouds gather, a storm blows in and hail starts to fall
I try to shelter the flower, to keep it safe and unharmed

I ache from bruises and cold

When the moonlight returns, I drop the flower
Thinking to watch petals blow away on the wind
But in wonder I stare at a complete crystal
That holds the same shape as the flower I held
Close to me, refined and glittering in light

The smell of jasmine and spice remains

IV. Eternal Breath of Dawn   Crystal Flowers by
Moonlight

Imagine a world where peace reigns
Where nature lives in harmony with us
Where all are acknowledged as worthy

See there's the river of change -
if you bathe in it you will become
the reflection of the truths of your soul
the broken mended, the lost made whole

It is a place where beauty does not blind
Where the wind brings voices singing hope
to you, and there is no need for money or
greed - there is no hunger, no pain

Imagine all this and even more
Could exist out there beyond
Hold the image in your mind
To help you when you open your eyes

I dream of flight, of fire, of freedom
of living as a bird; simply
to fly where the wind takes me
Trailing fire, golden flame
reborn from this life
Freedom to fly
with my soul
phoenix
cry

IV. Eternal Breath of Dawn   Phoenix Dreaming

At night as I try to find elusive sleep
I reach out to you, call your name
You take my hand, together we dream

With you I have seen dragons
Swam through a sea of stars
I met kings, lords and queens

No matter how long the day
Or how hard it was for me
I know you'll be there waiting

One day you'll leave me I know
But it'll be a while 'fore you go
Each dream we share is worth the pain
Of knowing that you will never remain

Floating, falling endlessly, completely at peace. I am no more than a whisper in the dark, a faint echo of a name remembered.

In the corner of every soul is darkness that light cannot penetrate, at the heart of that place is the truth of a life and beauty of a soul.

I was given wings for a reason
The stars are calling my name
Fate and destiny are winds to ride
Not slavers with whips and chains

I will dance upon moonbeams
Paint the night sky full of stars
The songs that we will ever sing
Keep us together when we're far

Comet trails are signs of our passing
Falling stars a chance to leave behind
All that pains and distresses you
Come with me now, come away and fly

For the stars are calling you - can you hear their silver song
Singing of dreams come true and a place you will always belong

They get lost in day dreams - of being able to wield a sword
To create flame and lightning from their fingertips, to heal
Oh how they dream of being able to heal - even at the cost
Of their own life, they would share it in a heartbeat to help

And they dream of fine clothing, of dragon scale armour
Of soft velvet and fancy jewels - they are royalty and power
A warrior, yet when they come back to themself, perhaps to
Dodge a pedestrian as they walk to the bus they are just themself

(It takes years before they realise that they can write these dreams
They can weave words to bring joy and hope and courage to many
Love is in their words, as they dance in marble halls their pen's strokes
Smoothly capturing their deal with the antagonist in vivid intense scrawl)

IV. Eternal Breath of Dawn   The Creators

I drift between the borders
Of asleep and awake
Wondering if your hand around me
Is just my wishful dreaming...

When I was sad, you caught my tears
Drew them away and threw them to the sky
Pulled down some stars and gave them to me
With your gentle fingers and loving lips
I thought I was dreaming, starry eyed
With you with me at my side
Swirling in a dance with no end
Until I awake from this dream in my head

...I choose to wake from this dreamlike state
Your hand does not melt away
This is real, and now I can feel
Happiness throughout lonely days

(I can always visit you in my dreams, but the reality is better, or so it seems)

IV. Eternal Breath of Dawn   Starry Eyed and Dreaming

Sitting at the piano fingers struggling to find the chords
Tears of frustration shimmer as I struggle with the words
Suddenly I feel her warmth at my back, lean fingers cover
Mine and music rings through the room, gentle as a lover

We play like this for minutes (hours) then he draws me to my feet
Somehow the music continues as we dance once more complete
In a moment of timeless communion I look into his eyes of gold
Then our joined hands are full of butterflies which we gently hold

She smiles and in her face are the words to a thousand stories
Together we lift our hands, releasing butterflies and worries
They fall back around us a glittering golden rain
When it vanishes from the ground, I am alone again

Left behind where he once stood is a crystal heart
As I touch it I hear him whisper "We're never far apart"
I take it in my hand, walk out past the hallway mirror old
Glance over, let out a gasp - my eyes now flecked with gold

IV. Eternal Breath of Dawn   Dancing with Muse

Small round
Window
Peering out to see
Endless horizon
The soft blue of bejewelled sea
And the perfect pink-tinged sky
Blend together with clouds
Reflecting grey-purple

What lays beyond
That horizon, I don't know
Maybe another time I'll fly there
Leave behind my worries and care
Lose myself in the endless horizon

Though I live in gilded cage
With no-one to spend my days
Imprisoned here by wicked mage
I can dream, and hope, and pray

I dream of flight, to soar
On wings of golden flame
to find where streams of music pour
Where life is lived without shame

I dream of fire, burning bright
Of phoenix tears that heal
Flame and water, mixing right
To be the light of justice's anvil

I dream of freedom, that elusive thing
To love, and laugh and delight
Where no-one says that I can't sing
Free to live my life in a land of light

I dream of flight, of fire, of freedom
Soaring beyond the bounds of my cage
Maybe one day those things will come
If there's a key smuggled in through a page

Once, a long time ago and far away, or so the story goes
There was a town of innocent and lovely folk – until evil bore
Down upon them, covering the sky and turning all day to night

And in this town was born a girl, given no name – to name
Someone was to give them worth, to give them worth was
To draw down the evil upon them, for the spirit was malice and greed

The girl grew tall, and strong – one day she ran far from her home
Found the light of day, she vowed in the dawn to survive and learn to
Fight that she might return and free her home from the malicious spirit

On her travels she learned of two long knives – one of bright fire and
The other of cold magic, so she set out upon a quest to find them, that
They might be the tools for her to bring peace and light back to her home

She travelled long, fought hard and grew weary but eventually the knives she found
With them in her hands, and the experiences gained she thought she would be able
To face the evil, and slay them – thus freeing her loved ones and their home,

Then perhaps gain a name, so she journeyed back to the place where night
Never ended, and as she walked along the edge of where the shadow touched she
Called out to the Malicious one, come and fight me – come and meet your doom

When the shadow appeared – this unctuous thing that had no true form
The girl trembled but drew forth her knives and set herself for the battle
Darkness closed around her, she blocked on instinct what could've been a fatal blow

Her weapons glowed with magic and fire, she wielded them with grace
The battle raged for hours – light grew in her, and the spirit was diminishing;
They would not let go so easily, and with a cunning plan, they begged for a rest

When she granted it – the evil surged and within the girl it vanished
Instantly she realised that she had been possessed – with a clarity
Quickly fading she took the knives she held, and plunged them into her heart
The creature died within her, she saw the dawn-light return, before
Pain overtook her, she closed her eyes and then was gone
But the village came out to where she lay and set for her a pyre

In their dancing joy they remember her sacrifice, and outside the gates

IV. Eternal Breath of Dawn   Dawn-Bringer

There stand a monument dedicated to the woman who gave her all for them
And they engraved thereon "Dawn-bringer", through death she obtained her name

IV. Eternal Breath of Dawn						Dawn-Bringer

Pretty music for my love,
You whisper my name
We splash ocean waves
Then twilight, quiet stars,
A yellow diamond ring
The truth you wish of I...

"Yes I will be queen with you my love"

And wedding bells burst in the refrain
Echoing through mountains
We dance in the dark
Under the stars

IV. Eternal Breath of Dawn   A Proposal

take my hand outstretched and my wings will shelter us
life's storms cannot touch you here, wrapped in my arms
shadows of what once-was and could-be's, come dance with me
we are queens and kings of times gone past, long lost family

IV. Eternal Breath of Dawn					The Fourth Day

See there upon a misty hill
The pale queen crying still
For her lord lost long ago
Who left her here, far below

Rain does not touch him now
the wind tangles only her hair
his name a scar upon her heart
the one who held her soul bare

Gone far beyond, where cares and hurts can't touch him
Surely the aching she feels will fade with passage of time
as of now the season brings tears, she welcomes the pain
for he is not forgotten while her voice speaks his name

IV. Eternal Breath of Dawn   Upon a Distant Hill

At the first streaks of dawn, the
Birds sing as light refracts on
Clouds bringing colour to the
Dark world waiting down below
Each hour unwinds allowing us to
Forget our cares and embrace the joy
Graceful is nature's dance around us
Happiness is the sound of pouring rain
In the night an international choir sings
Joyful, we find our voices and our hope
Kind hands support us when we falter
Loving us across sunrises and sunsets

Midnight finds us holding hands across oceans
Now when the dance takes us away, we will reunite
One day we know our feet will draw us once more to
Paths of words, of love and joy we walked before
Quietly we hum the songs shared between us
Remembering the way we found ourselves together -

Sorrow touches us, but it is shared and easier
To bear, the joys we share also because we are
United, one family of many parts; a garden
Verdant, bold and beautiful, always calling out
Welcome home to old family and new friends, no
Xenophobia, no judgement just grace, just love
You are special, you are precious and you are loved
Zeus himself will not tear us apart, nor will any endings

IV. Eternal Breath of Dawn   Endings

V.   In Loving Memory

- Soaring Free

Lost in night's dark abyss
A star flickers with despair
If only, it cries with no words
Disbelief visible behind crystal walls

In a mirror's reflection there's a man of words
Daring to dream of life's breath, of hope renewed
Together with me – we are twinned images
Who seek to colour the world in gold and blue

Through poetry and chat nights I must confess
A slight crush formed, for your soul was my mirror
These beautiful minds of you and I could create;
Did create and will go on forever to still create

If fate had dealt me pocket aces, I wouldn't be alone
You'd be here with your boundless understanding of what love is
What we had, *she'venyo*, is more precious than silver stars
Lost in a moment, with trembling hands, I light a candle

My fragile heart grew strong under your care
The sky of my heart became brighter than gold
We sung a duet without words that bridged oceans,
Spanned continents full of respect and love for others

The shadow lurker came in the night and stole you
Far away from your friends of the heart and soul

V. In Loving Memory   Soaring Free

But the joke's on him because you live on in us
We will preserve and honour your memory

I will catch you was the creed by which you lived
As you freed the soul who had been re-chained
I wove us a story, turned our souls into characters
An epic in motion for the one who inspired me most

On silver phoenix wings I soar - a flight of inspiration
You are the wind beneath my wings bearing me home

www.ingramcontent.com/pod-product-compliance
Lightning Source LLC
Chambersburg PA
CBHW060409090426
42734CB00011B/2274